flower sucker

Yost | *est. 1987*

Copyright © 2022 Alexandra Yost

All rights reserved.

ISBN: 9798468023716

contents *commence*

dedication
forward *definition*
big ideas — *in brief*

lust ....

>subtle
>heat wave
>the farm
>not anyone but someone
>the professor
>eat me
>big dumb crush (on you)
>free house
>the horniness of motherhood

love ....

>forgiven theft
>a mother's mass
>birth
>roadkill
>on men
>friendship on a monday
>damsel
>comedy of errors
>comforts
>morning after
>windowpane

contents *continue*

fear ....

>growth
>disassociate
>notable defeat
>journey home
>humor
>control
>the Beatles curse
>midnight larder

anger ....

>excuse me sorry to
>ever after
>namesake on the patio
>year of the rings
>ownership
>disappointment
>hindsight
>punchcard
>my parent's deck
>leaving love street
>saint johns letter

contents *conclude*

uncertainty ....

> any given day
> relationship portrait
> ebb &
> displaced
> ways of a modern ghost
> traffic meditation
> passive protector
> postpartum
> grocery store
> side effects
> deescalate

stillness ....

> reminders
> what's next
> friendship on a tuesday
> that kind of love
> bad capitalist
> feel good moments
> at the metal show
> drag
> habitat
> unoriginal sin
> awake
> soiled

an offering & acknowledgments

it's like papi said —

i'd rather have dear friends than ex-lovers

donut economy

forward

/ **fawr** - werd / *noun , action , choice*

1. direction in which one is pulled once a decision to move away from past is reached
2. an emphasis on progress over regression & stuckness
3. commitment to live an unknown future

origin story

big ideas — *in brief*

spent too long living inside the
violence of someone else's noise
and forgot how frightening it is
listening to one's own

been said already but i do like
how a shadow needs the light

and let the record show that i want to burn — turned ash like fellow trees and witches same in a messy transition *yes* but it's the potential usefulness of empty shelves that feels most overwhelming how many cycles of organ rearrangement does a mother go through in the process of rebirthing is a riddle to which no reasonable number is worth considering

it's bothersome how beautiful
our destruction has become

meanwhile honking birds fly high
sewing stitches in the sky

recommend letting yourself go
numb to the soothing drone
of honeycomb

boxing *it turns out* is much
like dancing except i have
replaced my partner
with an opponent

(not another) s-e-x poem

ever bury a joke within a joke to avoid explaining how you actually feel ?

ultimately we came together
to come apart

poems of *lust*

a good plum

subtle

bite me hard
on the neck
hit that spot
in my brain
that will cause me
to itch
for your touch
    again

heat wave

like this your lips
are nice — so salty

plus the butter &
good cheese
i notice are
more readily
spreadable

for this — at least
i am grateful

quail choir

the farm

a well timed slap

mouths that taste of each other

bottle sweat on butcher block

all mutually intoxicating in this

friendship born of sheets

the stillness of hot air

exhaled on many porches

life around croaks

twilight muttering blue

as time passes irrelevant

not anyone but someone

would you peel me an orange
please i want to see
your forearm made wet by zest
as fingers burst sweetness free

then hand me the bulk of it
so i can feel the weight and
make savory the segments
with a tangible service
of my willing anticipation

the professor

you said kissing

is like punctuation

with a comma comma comma

parentheses and

asterisk breath

then ellipses

and — oh

i've missed these conversations

eat me

so in this next scene i'm on my knees
 — *to what purpose*
we may dare to explore it
 — *in service or prayer*
but rest assured you are
 — *who are you*
here on this stage
 — *i'm not following*
sharing the moment
 — *not leading either*
spotlight / vigil / taste of unripe fruits
 — *one bite is all i need*

slut

big dumb crush (on you)

there's a video

like to watch it with no sound

imagining smack hush of drums

fluid motion of two arms

head tilted / chin lifting

and — there's a flamingo

just the head in the corner

above yours and *you are the song*

obvious though you don't want the attention

damn that energy it's — intoxicating

free house

it's the kind of place where
well kept husbands come
to leave the seat up
complain about women
with licking lips
oh the wives of others
their basketball skills veil to
penetrative commentary
she gets buckets — man
readjust
still the seat is
left up

the horniness of motherhood

it's there first thing
in the morning with
a surprise elbow to the tit

lurks at the park
sound of balls
on wet pavement hits

corner store clerk
passing bathroom keys
knows you've both cleaned up
someone else's piss

hilarious / inconvenient — at best

pump it

poems of *love*

the big squeeze

forgiven theft

i walk on nectar
        she says
jumping across the bed
and it's beautiful

i sit
and type
and paint the world
inside her open mind

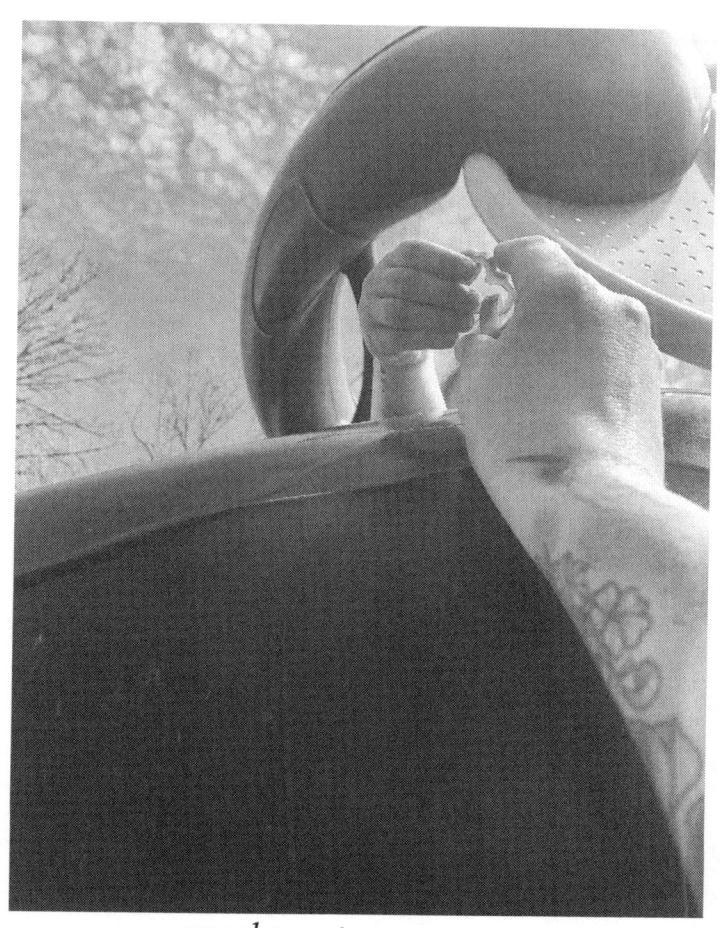

rascal monster

a mother's mass

on sundays i cry
like a worshiper caught
tears instantly crust
as you ask me to be
a cave — i oblige & my jaw
unhinged swallows the moment whole
you dissolve on my tongue *slowly*
two days of this feast
a wafer memory

birth

soon as i let you out i let you in
primal grab *dark* in pitch
as your steady heart
hushed those attending
like how did you not
flinch when all muscle surrounding
contracted in force enough
to break open a body mine
your choice to arrive prudent
reminds us of purpose
of limits of duty to service
the parts we've been left with

roadkill

observing raccoons bloated
strewn about the freeway
any day now any day

waiting for "the one"
some-one to bear witness
speeding by *just* trying to get there

not too fast   *someone — one day*

going to show you

    my everything / my emptiness
    exploding chest / whatever's left

we'll get there
someone — one day

on men

rarely judge a book
by its cover anymore
because really — i just like
reading too much
to not try cracking
another and another
or one other to be sure

friendship on a monday

post nut clarity — at work
walk in with *sex face sex hair*
sex under fingernails
washes hands again as
teacher teacher no one yells
lacking in regrets — none
feeling delayed satisfaction hum
to the swan's song sung right
snapping into place a pace
a moment to touch on and
with whiteboard written prompt
root of suffering will dry erase

damsel

damn fool

falling in & out of

— split like head

hitting cement

making statements

of heart knowing minds

soon catch up but

feels good in the

— *moment*

yeah huh ?

comedy of errors

face lit by cell phone screen
and that's when you know
you've made it
12:39 AM swiping on fish
men with big fish
but mostly the fish
counting scales like wishes
hoping all appeals go unrequited
so you have stories not futures
to sell

scream

necking

comforts

swaddled in a layer of shared sweat from
armpits linked — and i am safe

touched with a tongue tracing seashell likeness
of an ear — and i am calm

grabbed at the ass by a hand of respectful boundaries
and i am — delighted

morning after

between these snores
there are breaths taken / afraid to be given

between them lies a pause
where unasked questions shoulder our burdens

between — where
tiniest of dreams are chased
wanted yet stubbornly unseen

holding no memories
having never been conceived

windowpane

ancient iron crosses glass
not once but twice in the line of sight

pretty in that *troublesome* kind of way

it's then i realize we are like a story
— the kind that ends

poems of *fear*

till death do us part

growth

why make yourself small
to fit inside the space given
you are not small
we are not meant for boxes
i am big like a fungus
spreading blooms across the surface
of what lived here once before
— repurposed

disassociate

fingers smell like
come & nail polish remover
fresh coat now — a darker blue
shade called *urban*
makes me want to puke a little
rinsed dishes in the shower
because sink's inferior but
tomorrow's gonna show no matter
how many cotton balls
i swallow
so —

notable defeat

hey so
i love you like *big*

like a wash of color
like an indistinguishable odor
like a hammer
like the dust leftover

i love you like the tingle
of a hungry hunter huge
or seldom worn suit

i'd tell you as much
if the thought of admitting
didn't render me totally mute

truth spray

journey home

driving seventy five there's
a limit no one abides
sudden dread manifested
spider snuck into my boot
oxblood and laced eight high
swear i would feed it every limb
bargaining for your life

humor

it's funny because
there's a hornet nest
in my freezer and
though it's no metaphor
i can't think of one
to better sum up all
my earthly fears either

control

daughter gets first
bee sting & here i am
midnight hovering over her tiny frame
checking exhalations
as if there were *anything*
i could do to stop
life from unmasking itself
like this again

higher mama

the Beatles curse

shooting pistachios like
oysters at the breakfast counter
you're naked asking *why why why*
i'm raw
this song always makes me —

& the ants were everywhere this morning
so i killed them like a tyrant

finding a groove we drink our juice
sour diluted / day bringing / boys are singing
music makes it better worse
of course

midnight larder

lone hot dog in the fridge sits
wrapped in meat sweats
shriveled judgment on a shelf of
cold indulgence

oh i want you
see you / need you
oh to be rid of this
hunger / sickness
      for good

poems of *anger*

dull blade / deep cuts

excuse me sorry to

i don't mean to be
a bother but imbedded
between the treads on
your left sole there
are a few pieces of me and
yes i know they make you taller but
with due respect to past
agreements vowed faithful *tried to keep*
they ultimately belong to me and
are much needed parts for
future ability to be
complete

ever after

disgusting you are
words spat out bitter
tongues of two
to the pith leaving
slug trails across face
an Object once adored
now named *selfish*
for standing up taller
than in decades before

namesake on the patio

She said

It's Alexandra
I'm not a city
Never been a city
I'm not
— a city

and she's right because
though we be vast with
structures intact
adding extra line dot i
ascribes unnecessary
femininity to a woman
whose name seeks
no apology

cheers (bitch)

year of the rings

punched a hole in my face
just to prove it was mine
— Man said
take yoga breaths
as the needle goes deep and
why not — because pain is fleeting
the gift is seeing Anger as Love
that hasn't been to therapy yet

ownership

never shaving
she wears bruises
on legs sexy
edges fading
like an awkward badge
awarded for reckless
car seat choices

a special memento
for the *fuck it*
of the moment

disappointment

is a fig

straight from the fridge

whose guts are

tender cold & lacking in juices

with pungent smell of — not

hindsight

ok so it's twenty twenty *right*
and they're a gas station candy bar
not the fuel needed *really*
more like convenience within reach
tasty — a want to fill whatever itched
brought to makeshift table by another
from whom their taking makes
Man's attempt to claim anything
a total *my bad bro* mistake

punchcard

had the abortion

then went to brunch

stood in line — so Portland

fucking millennials amassed and i

was just being

the *responsible*

idiot

my parent's deck

but why am i

getting cussed out

by flower suckers

buzzing busy bodies

on bright and boastful wings

They the watchers

of sour grapes greening sweet

chide with tiny beaks

as slender tongues

dip taste & vibe on

uncut floral ecstasy

leaving love street

if timed right the birthday
blooms will be dead by
valentine's and
smelling of summer memories
yard debris / grilling meats
grammy throwing snails
into the —
crack goes a shell as little dancing
feet hit bricks moving
to whatever beat and
now we exit a chapter incomplete

saint johns letter

so what's the plan then
hop state lines to bury face in grit under bridges
invest daily in street bird grudges
buy a yellow moped *just to fit in* then fall
for some pisces *probably*
down by the river
one who likes sports too much
but still knows how to fuck
wait — actually that
sounds like a lot of fun

poems of *uncertainty*

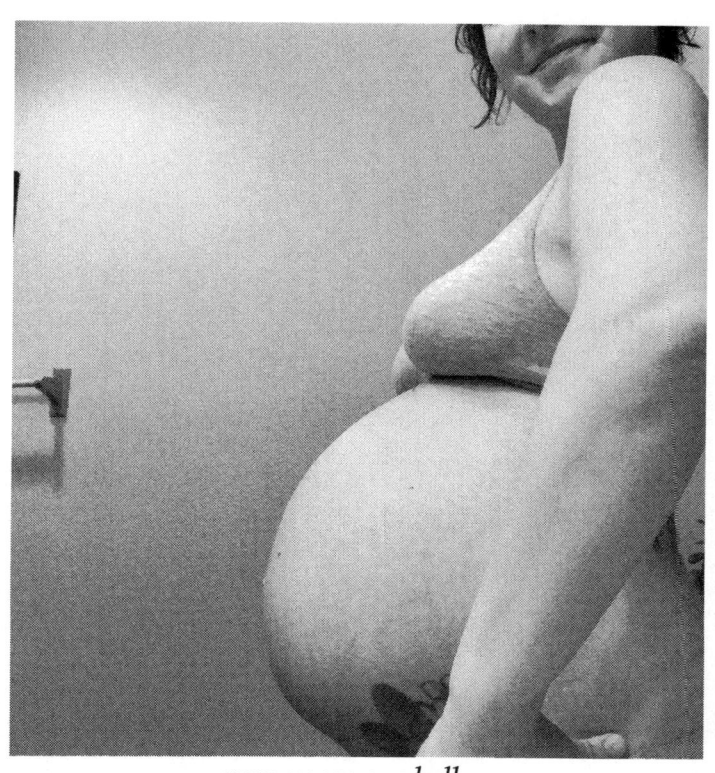

new years eve belly

any given day

sometimes i forget to drink water
sometimes i remember to breathe
sometimes my hands make shapes so objectively rude
that we argue until embarrassed they go back to sleep

sometimes a heartbeat is the loudest sound we create
sometimes i savor the silence of an aftertaste

sometimes the thoughts don't have purpose
tickling them free with flicks of my tongue
they tumble combinations
imperfect on the dismount

relationship portrait

young woman selects a course
feels wanted *inspired*
assumes shared cost and expectation to excel
lessons begin — choosing bold color palette
pushing stiff hairs into submission
gathered and by metal bound at the tip *disjointed*
making persistent strokes on
joyful wood that *splinters* triumphant pain
years pass / perspective gained — but the subject
moldy *forgotten* in a bowl

ebb &

      clear glass bottle
      half empty
       still thirsty
studiously so
      acting on thrust &
      nary a thought
      could escape slight
         dampness
         upon seeing
an elbow bare
    not so recently
    having burst free
    from its sleeve
    like a
    professor giving out
      last —
        wondering if there
        isn't perhaps
      one left
    for me

displaced

rearranged the furniture
productive yes
but still horny & possibly more so

punched a purchased thing
door frame hung caloric purging
but still anxious — text pending

dishes sudsed & drying
pile is perfect
but still no room for anything

nails painted light
like tiny pills matching
but still if poetry is medicine

then life is so exquisitely *fucked*

ways of a modern ghost

home early — keys dangling
mail gripped by teeth
threshold within reach and
some men bring flowers
but you with the vinegars
packaged & sugar cane sweet
i walked *so hard* into the wall
missing a door — clearly wide open
but couldn't see

traffic meditation

flexed palms syncopate
on steering wheel rounds
making dumb eyes at truck drivers
while on freeway entrance waiting

maybe today won't be counted
towards the sum of a greater mess

maybe tomorrow can just admit
it's never going to exist

maybe blisters heal uneven
because time has a duty to remind
us of the pain we will inflict

passive protector

the dog i wonder

how many meals he made

face licking tears *kissed off*

the mass of his body

positioned as shield

to all danger

occasionally humping a lover's leg

exposing belly in

subsequent submissive behavior

allowed because there never existed any

conditions to the way in which

he loved

a hard world simple

his majesty

postpartum

at the farmers' market
you're six days fresh
vendor *friendly* asks if i tore
any flesh and — well

his hands know the soil so
line of questioning
a presumption of respect

paid for the produce
& answered an honest
— yes

grocery store

handwritten list

aisle walking dead

come hungry / leave horny

why so friendly

just take my money

crossing the street and

children toss dildos

all tied up with string

hung pretty because sneakers

— too obvious an accessory

side effects

black daisy top scoop necked and
dressed down for the party then body
ruptures to release one million tiny butterflies
atomized in blue / limbs immobilized
aflame on the inside & so *doctor doctor* we adjust

in hopes that tomorrow
will be better brighter
new

deescalate

frozen to the ankle in
tundra of shared trauma
frostbitten digits
ache back to blood
flowing like no bird does
the urge to *flee fight fuck*
comes on quick
not frightened yet but
flightless yes
stuck to a place
where all prey sit
— awaiting silence

poems of *stillness*

morning commute

reminders

two dead birds

waiting in the driveway

gravel crunch

you ask questions

quiet scooping *once twice*

lightness of lifeless

so little left

lift the lid *once twice*

municipal bin a new nest

not waste but

in transition nonetheless

what's next

homeward step and holding breath
because gnats are out
to mate in clumps of disorder
while beyond the path
daisies push faces up pretty
signaling to hollow bones above
presence of recent death
and chain link perspectives
bring end to a journey
meant to be many miles longer

friendship on a tuesday

circling the blocks together
— *she asked for water i gave her a bowl*
side eye but judgment reserved
— *it had a handle so pretty solid third date move no ?*
nods of agreement / looks for approval
(oh i'd say something if you were being an asshole)
droplets fall harder
— *hey a rainbow*
takes picture / looks uncomfortable
time passes damp
— *where the fuck's my car*
thoroughly soaked in a feeling that
i hope will never pass

human supreme

that kind of love

taste of water from the garden hose

slightly warmed — not unpleasant

like a big pile of dirt *delivered*

dumped in the driveway

heaped & potential if spread out

the smell *mulched* overwhelms until

a hunger and thirst reeking of *just*

out of reach — inspires the recipe

always meant to be incomplete

bad capitalist

as an ingredient — it isn't profitable
the kindness required to
propagate it well enough to thrive
cannot be commodified

— and besides
i'd never allow anything
to leave my kitchen *unloved*
in the first place

feel good moments

babe where's my wallet
above the toilet *what*
oh right — because
there's no better time
to check your credit score
than when taking a
massive dump

at the metal show

better angel thinks himself
Devil — says

fucking me is
not an act of mutual aid
but wiping floor sweat ?
makes a pit safe for all
well *that* most certainly is

then passing the cigarette
encircles me in bed

a large irishman

drag

the thing with

cigarettes is *i'm jealous*

convenience of tightly rolled

vices in my pocket

dragging perpetually postcoital puffs

in public nodding / half listening

stranger lovers pull closer

still —

seems an exhale that satisfying

would be enough

habitat

back stoop occupied by black silk boxers

a matching bra worn — all old and comfortable

inhabited by body lifted / smoke rising on the exhale

puff puff no one to pass to — instead staring dead eyed

desperate and trying to soften an expectation to always

be well

unoriginal sin

the apple eater

smacks

in bed making

chomps loud

turning the page

a hotel bible

distressed

— shhh

Eve says *quiet*

i love this part

it's about my ex

awake

a tickling of walrus whiskers
and an ache of lion yawns

a duty of hummingbird heartbeats
and a cadence of vermin feet

plus an impotence of jellyfish stings
and a flicking of insect abdomens

all things to ponder
while staring at the ceiling
open eyed and dreaming

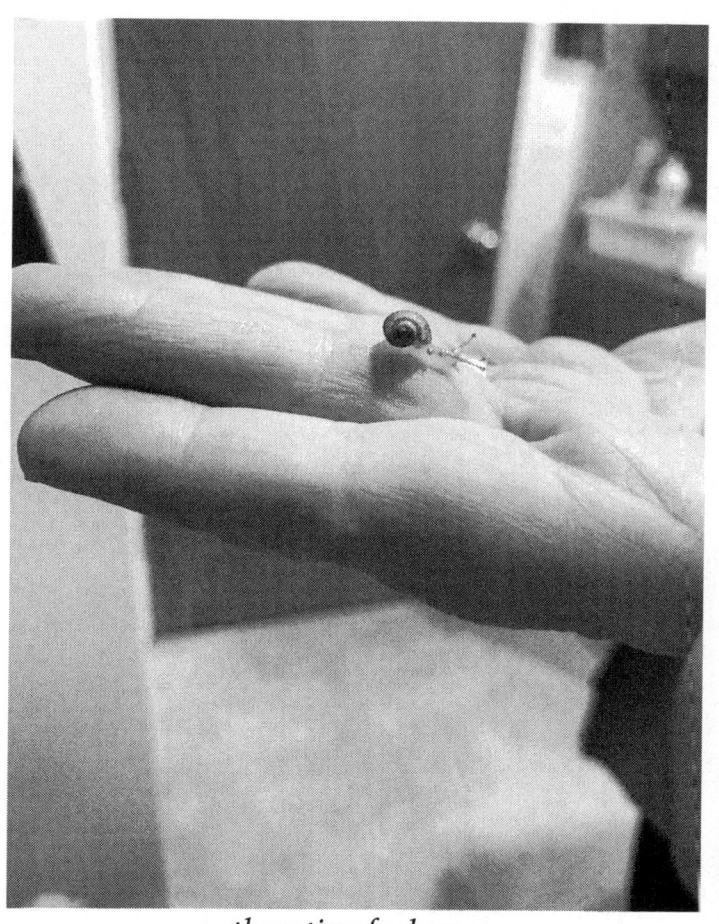

these tiny fuckers

soiled

had that dream
showed up at the house
naked *but socks*
holding the heart
of an onion sweet

you had two
fistfuls of basil
smelled great but
said i didn't have
what you need
so i left
now with bare feet

& it wasn't awkward
or anything

in lieu of closure
an offering

let me show you how i love you
i will poach this piece of fish
pull her gently from a bath aromatic
and together upon the bones
you & i can make a wish

acknowledgments

To the *Folks* teachers of a naked truth; love is unconditional. To the *Child* flip me always you righteous babe. To the *Sisterhood* my moon and my rocks. To the *Family* my blood and of whose bones I am sculpted. To the *Dog* rest easy you fantastic beast of occasional burden. To the *Men* my dearest princes of cats. To the *Bar* my home and sanctuary, in your chaos I find peace.

mom jokes

because endings seldom begin like this

let the imagined scent of a shadow fart

honor our time together spent

                                          XO